COLONIAL PEOPLE

The Blacksmith

CHRISTINE PETERSEN

 **Marshall Cavendish**
Benchmark
New York

Other Marshall Cavendish Offices:

Marshall Cavendish International (Asia) Private Limited, 1 New Industrial Road, Singapore 536196 • Marshall Cavendish International (Thailand) Co Ltd. 253 Asoke, 12th Flr, Sukhumvit 21 Road, Klongtoey Nua, Wattana, Bangkok 10110, Thailand • Marshall Cavendish (Malaysia) Sdn Bhd, Times Subang, Lot 46, Subang Hi-Tech Industrial Park, Batu Tiga, 40000 Shah Alam, Selangor Darul Ehsan, Malaysia

Marshall Cavendish is a trademark of Times Publishing Limited

All websites were available and accurate when this book was sent to press.

Library of Congress Cataloging-in-Publication Data

Petersen, Christine.
The blacksmith / by Christine Petersen.
p. cm. — (Colonial people)
Includes bibliographical references and index.
Summary: "Explore the life of a colonial blacksmith and his importance to the community, as well as everyday life, responsibilities, and social practices during that time"—Provided by publisher.
ISBN 978-0-7614-4799-3
1. Blacksmithing—United States—History—17th century—Juvenile literature.
2. Blacksmithing—United States—History—18th century—Juvenile literature.
3. Blacksmiths—United States—History—17th century—Juvenile literature.
4. Blacksmiths—United States—History—18th century—Juvenile literature.
5. United States—History—Colonial period, ca. 1600–1775—Juvenile literature. I. Title.
TT220.P48 2010
682.9—dc22
2009024861

Editor: Christine Florie
Publisher: Michelle Bisson
Art Director: Anahid Hamparian
Series Designer: Kay Petronio

Expert Reader: Paul Douglas Newman, Ph.D., Department of History, University of Pittsburgh at Johnstown

Photo research by Marybeth Kavanagh

The photographs in this book are used by permission and through the courtesy of:
North Wind Picture Archives: 4, 16, 21, 27; The Colonial Williamsburg Foundation: 9, 18, 37; The Image Works: Mary Evans Picture Library, 10; Alamy: Witold Skrypczak, 13; Photolibrary: The Print Collector, 22; The Granger Collection: 25, 38, 41; Getty Images: MPI, 30

Printed in Malaysia (T)
1 3 5 6 4 2

CONTENTS

ONE

Building the Colonies

When English colonists arrived on American soil in 1607, their goal was to spend a few years claiming land and valuable resources from the New World. These ambitious men needed help to accomplish their goal. Many Englishmen were picked from jails and poorhouses to serve as a source of inexpensive labor in America. Smaller numbers of skilled workers were hired to join the colonial expedition. Very much in need were **craftsmen**, such as blacksmiths, who were essential in building their new settlement.

Settling the Land

American Indians had tamed much of the land along the coast of the Atlantic Ocean. They cleared trees around their villages and set up farms on the open ground. But outside these areas the forest

When the Pilgrims landed at Plymouth, Massachusetts, in the early 1600s, the first task at hand was to build their homes. Their tools were made and repaired by the blacksmith.

seemed to go on forever. The colonists had to carve out their place within it, building everything from scratch.

Their first task was to put up houses and forts. They also needed to clear land for farms. Colonists brought a variety of metal tools from England, including saws, hammers, axes, and plows. But months of use left them dull, splintered, and chipped. A man could sharpen his tools by rubbing a hard stone against the blade. But he had no way to mend a broken tool. Only the blacksmith could solve that problem. The blacksmith was a trained craftsman who worked with iron and steel. He used fire to heat these metals and a hammer to **smite**, or pound, them into shape. In his hands, plain pieces of iron and steel became useful objects. Broken or worn items could be remade almost like new.

Everyone Needs Iron

Colonists' homes, barns, and workshops were filled with objects made of iron and steel. They cooked on iron broilers and scooped water from buckets using iron spoons. The farmer cut his dinner with a steel knife, and he shaved with a razor made of that same hard metal. He threw hay to his cow with an iron pitchfork. And an iron bell hung from the cow's neck.

At first the colonists relied on supplies of metal from England.

The First American Blacksmith

The first permanent colony in America was established at Jamestown, along the coast of Virginia. Approximately 150 men arrived in 1607, eager to make their fortunes in the New World. None of the colonists had ever worked as farmers. They had a hard time raising food in the new environment. A local drought added to their challenges. Within months they began to die of starvation, illness, and injuries received during fights with the American Indians who lived in the region.

Among those first colonists was a blacksmith named James Read. He survived the first few frightening months of colonial life in good health. But the blacksmith almost lost his life another way. When Jamestown's first governor was arrested and replaced, Read stood up in his defense. He argued with the new governor and hit him. Read was given the death sentence as punishment.

Even if his action was wrong, James Read knew that his death would be devastating for Jamestown. The community needed a blacksmith. He gained his freedom by telling the court that another colonist had planned to attack the government. The second man was put to death, and James Read survived to work as a blacksmith in Jamestown for fifteen years.

Items made of iron or steel were produced there and shipped to the colonies, where they could be purchased in shops. Local blacksmiths spent most of their time on repairs.

But England's own supplies of iron were limited. The colonists wasted no time looking for iron in America. Colonists at Jamestown, Virginia, found iron in marshlands near their fort soon after they arrived in 1607. This **bog iron** had been carried down from the mountains by rushing streams, and it had become trapped in the still marshes. The people used rakes to dig clumps of the metal out of the murky water.

Bog iron is actually an **ore**. It was useless to the blacksmith until the metal it contained had been removed and made pure. This job was called **smelting**, and an expert called the ironmaster oversaw the work. Chunks of ore were placed into small furnaces and heated over a **charcoal** fire. At very high temperatures, pieces of iron in the rock combined with carbon released by the burning charcoal. This caused the iron to separate from the rest of the rock and fall in soft clumps to the bottom of the furnace. The ironmaster gathered the hot iron and hammered it to remove air, as well as any remaining rock or dirt. Finally, the clumps were reheated and hammered into long bars of pure metal, which was called wrought iron. Blacksmiths preferred wrought iron because it was strong,

In the re-created colonial town of Williamsburg, Virginia, blacksmiths smelt bog iron.

durable, and could go many years without rusting. Yet it was also an easy metal to shape. When the blacksmith held a wrought iron bar in the fire, it became soft enough to bend, twist, or cut.

The first successful ironworks in the colonies was established in 1644 beside the Saugus River in Massachusetts. Its **blast furnace** could produce a ton of iron in each load—twenty times as much as the older furnaces had held. One owner reported a huge success: "[T]he furnace now runs seven tons per week."

During the mid–1700s iron ore was mined from the ground. Here it is loaded onto horse-drawn carts.

By the 1730s colonists had begun to mine iron ore from the ground in addition to collecting bog iron. A large proportion of the smelted iron was shipped back to England.

As the colonies grew, the blacksmith's access to American iron became increasingly important. He provided the tools and materials that helped colonists farm the land, build homes, and construct ships that carried goods to and from England. It's no wonder that the blacksmith was considered an essential part of every colonial community.

TWO

The Blacksmith's Helpers

In paintings the blacksmith is often shown as a large and burly man. He seems to have unmatched strength, lifting his heavy, long-handled sledgehammer over and over through the day. But even the most powerful blacksmith could never manage his workshop, called a smithy, alone.

Learning the Trade

The blacksmith's oldest son might dream of becoming a ship's captain or a minister. He might show promise as a teacher or be a talented artist. Yet no matter what other skills he possessed, this boy almost always followed in his father's footsteps. By the age of ten or twelve he began to help around the shop. The boy was given simple tasks at first—splitting and hauling wood, filling the charcoal bin, putting away tools, and cleaning out the massive blacksmith's **forge** fireplace. He was sent around town on errands and assigned to keep the shop tidy.

The blacksmith's son was eventually allowed to maintain the forge fire and to pump the **bellows**, a device used to blow air into the flames. If the boy did well, the blacksmith began to let him work with metals at the forge. The child would start by making small, simple objects such as nails. It took many tries to learn to heat the metal evenly, pound it out, and make straight nails that would not break. The boy practiced making nails of different

It was not unusual for the son of a blacksmith to follow in his father's footsteps and learn the trade.

sizes, with perfect points and differently shaped heads. As he grew more confident, he learned from his father how to hammer, bend, and **weld** many other useful objects.

The blacksmith might also agree to train boys other than his son. These were called **apprentices**. Apprenticeship usually lasted about five years. The boy signed a contract agreeing to behave well and to work hard for the blacksmith. The blacksmith promised to pass on his skills and to provide a home for the boy. Parents often paid to have their sons apprenticed, and basic schooling was included in the contract. The blacksmith taught his apprentices to read, write, and do arithmetic. He understood that this knowledge was as important as any of the metalworking skills the boys would learn. The blacksmith used arithmetic every day in his work to calculate weight, size, and angles. He also needed to do "Merchants accompts"—accounting—to accurately charge his customers and to pay his own bills.

Apprenticeship was rarely an easy time for a boy. He was considered a servant, expected to do anything the master blacksmith asked. Apprentices sometimes ran away, and the master blacksmith believed it was his right to punish them for bad behavior. But apprenticeship was the best way to learn a good trade in colonial America, and most boys settled into the work.

Tug of War

Blacksmiths were so important in colonial America that communities often competed to get their services. In 1650 John Prentice completed his apprenticeship with a blacksmith in Roxbury, Massachusetts. He married the next year and worked for two years as a journeyman in Roxbury. Then he began to look for a place to set up his own shop. The residents of Hadley, Massachusetts, soon offered Prentice a job. But the people of New London, Connecticut, also wanted his services. They offered him land, a house and shop, and a supply of iron and steel to get him started. John Prentice was no fool. He signed a contract with New London and prospered as the town's blacksmith for many years.

The Journeyman Blacksmith

When his apprenticeship was complete, a young blacksmith was given a set of new tools to show that he was now a journeyman. The journeyman had skills, but he had to gain experience in applying them. He would travel through the countryside and provide blacksmithing services wherever they were needed.

The journeyman might also work as a paid assistant in an established blacksmith shop. He was trusted to take over many jobs in the smithy. With one glance at the day's list of jobs, the journeyman knew exactly which tools to set out and how to prepare the fire. He usually kept an eye on the apprentices, as well. But his most important work was done beside the forge, alongside the blacksmith. The two men could work together on a project without speaking, using simple signals and a familiar rhythm of hammering.

The journeyman worked from dawn to dusk, every day except Sunday. In 1760 his income averaged fifteen shillings a week—about twenty dollars in today's currency. If he saved well, the journeyman could eventually set up his own shop. He looked for a community in need of help, married, and settled in to his life's work. Before long he might have a son to sweep the floors of his smithy and continue the tradition that kept the colonies growing.

A journeyman assists a blacksmith at the smithy's forge.

THREE

In the Smithy

Like most colonial craftsmen, the blacksmith had a short distance to travel between work and home. His smithy was a large, open room. It was either attached to his house or located in a building on his property. The smithy was filled with tools and supplies from floor to ceiling. But the first thing any visitor noticed was the forge. This massive fireplace filled the center of the smithy floor. It was the heart of the blacksmith's world.

The forge looked nothing like a household fireplace. It was usually constructed of wood with a lining of hardened dirt and clay that absorbed heat but would not catch on fire. The fire burned inside a square hearth that was larger than a dining table and stood as high as a man's hips. A boxlike hood hung from the chimney to cover the hearth. This arrangement pulled smoke up the chimney, allowing those who worked inside to breathe comfortably and to see what they were doing.

When the smithy was opened each day, every worker went right to his assigned job. The apprentice piled fresh wood and charcoal into boxes beside the forge. The blacksmith or journeyman was responsible for starting a fire in the forge. He began by cleaning the previous day's ashes from the hearth. In their place he made a tent-shaped pile of dry wood, with a handful of paper-thin wood shavings at the bottom. The colonial blacksmith had no matches or lighter fluid with which to start a fire. Instead he used small pieces

A new day at the smithy begins with firing up the forge and hammering at the anvil.

Fuel for the Fire

Coal was the most important fuel in Europe from the 1300s onward. Colonists preferred to use charcoal, which could be made from local supplies of wood. A charcoal-making furnace was simple. Cut wood was stacked in a pile, and the pile was covered with sand. The woodpile was lit through a hole in the sand and allowed to burn slowly for several days. The result was dense, black chunks of charcoal. When these cooled, they could be shipped from place to place and stored for long periods. They lit easily and burned for a long time.

of flint and steel. He held the steel in one hand and quickly struck the flint against it. When he did this just right, a spark was made. A few sparks were usually enough to set the wood shavings aflame. Soon the wood was crackling, and a warm fire leaped in the hearth. More wood was added throughout the day, but most of the heat came from charcoal.

Preparing to Work

Once the forge was ready, the blacksmith checked his schedule for the day. He might already have customers waiting for repairs or a list of jobs to be done. Whether the projects were big or small, he always organized his tools before beginning to work. The blacksmith's long workbench next to the forge was like an office worker's desk. He laid all his tools out on the bench so that he could reach them while working.

The blacksmith did not wear gloves, for then his fingers would be too thick and clumsy. Instead, he used tongs to hold a piece of iron or steel in the fire. When the metal was hot enough, he pulled it from the fire and turned to place it on his **anvil**. This heavy iron block had a flat top covered in a layer of steel that could withstand years of pounding and heat. A large blacksmith shop might have several anvils. Some weighed more than a grown man—up to 250 pounds. To keep the anvil steady, the smith mounted it atop a wooden stump that was sunk into the floor of the smithy.

The blacksmith used large, heavy hammers called sledges to slowly pound out the iron. Flat objects were hammered on the smooth surface of the anvil. The anvil also had a pointed horn on one end. This could be used to make bends in the metal. Round items, such as bowls and spoons, were shaped on yet another anvil called a **swage**. Anvils of this type were steel or wooden blocks cut in various shapes. A swage served as a mold around which the blacksmith pounded hot metal until it achieved the desired form.

When he finished working on an object, he placed it on the floor to cool.

The blacksmith had to keep an eye on his fire throughout the day. He added charcoal and wood now and then and shifted the pieces among the ashes to keep the heat even. When he wanted to increase the temperature of the fire, the blacksmith had another option—to use the bellows. This device consisted of three large, balloon-shaped planks of wood laid on top of each other. Leather bindings connected the pieces and allowed them to open and close like an accordion. The bellows was laid on its side and mounted on a frame behind the forge. The pointed end was tipped with a nozzle, which fit into a hole in the chimney. On a large forge, the bellows might be 8 feet long.

A blacksmith uses his sledge to make nails at the anvil.

The smith worked the bellows by hooking a chain between the bottom plank and a lever that was hung above. When he pulled on the lever, the planks of the bellows squeezed together. Air was

Forced air from the bellows (left) creates a very hot fire in the forge.

forced out of the bellows and into the forge. These gusts of air caused the fire to burn hotter. The blacksmith pumped the bellows before placing iron in the fire. It took only a few pumps to turn a gentle fire into a roaring blaze.

Ending the Day

The blacksmith completed his work in late afternoon. After the last job he carefully inspected all of his tools. He rubbed oil into the metal to prevent rust from forming. Small chips or breaks were patiently filed down. Blacksmith's tools that had been used to the point of breaking were added to the pile of work for the next day. All other tools were hung back in their places on the walls. He also made sure that the smithy was swept to remove the day's mess of ash and metal flakes.

Each night the blacksmith had to decide what to do with the forge. In good weather he might douse it with water and start fresh in the morning. On cold and wet nights, however, he often chose to leave a few coals, nestled in a bed of ashes, burning on the hearth. Their heat would last through the night and greet him when he opened the smithy the next day.

FOUR

Everyone Needs the Blacksmith

Iron and steel were the most common metals used in colonial America, and eventually everyone needed the services of the blacksmith. Colonists rarely needed a sign to find the smithy. The ringing sound of his hammer carried far along the road, and a gray plume of smoke rose from the chimney of his forge. A traveler might find a blacksmith shop almost anywhere he went—in the smallest village, on a distant farm, or in the largest city.

In the Village

A colonist might hold many jobs—innkeeper, lawyer, minister, or craftsman. No matter his profession, he almost always kept a farm as well. This was a source of food for his family and additional income in hard times. Most farming tools were made from wood but had iron parts for cutting. The hoe and plow both had iron

In farms, cities, or small villages, a blacksmith's shop could always be found.

blades that turned the soil to prepare it for planting. In autumn the farmer brought out his harvesting implements: cradle, sickle, and scythe. The wickedly curved blades on these tools were dangerous, but they made it much easier to cut down tall crops such as wheat. The farmer collected wood with an ax or saw and dug holes with a shovel or spade. His cart, wagon, and harnesses also had metal parts, which got heavy wear along the rough colonial roads in all kinds of weather. Most farmers could make simple repairs, but they relied on the local blacksmith for the large jobs. Every farmer kept a pile of broken tools and took them in to be worked on, a few at a time. Sometimes this was done in winter, when farmers had time to stop and inspect their equipment.

A variety of iron objects was also important to the colonial housewife. She bought cast iron pots and pans, long-handled soup ladles, and iron eating utensils. These were so sturdy that they often lasted for years. When they finally broke, the housewife made a visit to the blacksmith, who usually could weld the parts back together. First he flattened out the broken ends of each piece. Using tongs, he held the two pieces in the fire until the iron turned white-hot. At this stage the metal was very soft. Turning to his anvil, the blacksmith hammered the two softened pieces together. The hot metal fused into one piece. He made a few careful hits with his hammer to smooth out the edge. After the mended item cooled, it looked as good as new and could often be used for many more years.

The colonial housewife used many iron utensils. This woman stirs dinner cooked in an iron pot with an iron spoon.

On the Plantation

Most colonial farms were small, and all the work was done by the landowner and his family. But some colonists could afford to buy large plantations—and they needed many workers. A local blacksmith might be hired to live and work on the plantation.

Or he might be brought over from Europe as an indentured servant. **Indenture** was a system in which a farmer or other colonist paid to bring workers and their families across the sea. The person who paid provided food and a place for the new Americans to live. In return, the worker owed several years of unpaid labor. A man was promised land and tools to begin his new life in freedom after completing his indenture.

Many Europeans came to the colonies through the system of indenture. It was a hard life. Indentured servants worked long hours and had little time off to rest. They suffered from a variety of diseases, and some simply died of exhaustion. On average, only 10 percent of indentured servants in the American colonies reached their goal of freedom.

Some of the first Africans in the colonies were also indentured servants. In 1619 a Dutch slave ship docked in Jamestown, Virginia. The captain traded twenty African prisoners for supplies. The Africans, who were taken on as indentured servants, later were given land as free people. This practice would not last long, however. Slavery soon became an important way of providing labor on growing farms. American Indians were enslaved in some places, and more slaves were brought from Africa. A farmer could save money by using the talents of his slaves to help run the plantation. Trusted slaves were trained in many crafts—carpentry, shoemaking, weaving, and more. The slave blacksmith shoed horses and fixed broken farm tools. He worked with the leatherworker to make harnesses for the horses, and he forged the handheld irons that women used to smooth clothes. His job was very much like that of the white blacksmith—except that the money

I'll Meet You at the Smithy

The local smithy was more than a workshop. It was a warm haven on a cold day, and the blacksmith's hammer made noise that allowed people to talk privately. As they waited to pick up or drop off an item, adults took the chance to share the latest news and to argue over politics. They made business deals and worried over the weather.

Children came to eavesdrop on the grown-up talk. Sometimes the blacksmith allowed them to help at the grindstone, a machine used to sharpen tools. The large circular stone was mounted on a wooden frame and attached to an axle so it could spin. The child's first job was to drip water onto the stone. This made it turn more smoothly. When the child began to crank the handle, the blacksmith placed the tool on the stone. Sound filled the air as the metal was sharpened.

for his services went to his master, and he could be sold to another farmer at any time, usually without his family.

In the Cities

Most colonial cities grew up alongside rivers or ocean bays, where goods could easily be transported by boat. The colonists soon began using wood from the lush local forests to build ships. For this reason, a city blacksmith might prefer to set up his shop near the shipyards. He was guaranteed plenty of work, for ships used hundreds of iron parts. The blacksmith made all of the **shipwright**'s tools. He hammered out thousands of iron rivets, which held the planks of the deck together. He even forged the massive chains and anchors that kept heavy ships from drifting.

This shipwright's tools were crafted by the town's blacksmith.

The blacksmith also found plenty of work in city neighborhoods. His city customers were likely to be craftsmen. The mason needed special hand tools for laying bricks and plastering. Carpenters used many different implements, such as adzes, augers, and axes, when cutting and shaping wood—as well as thousands of square-headed nails. Carriage makers sometimes hired blacksmiths to work in their shops. These blacksmiths forged metal tires to surround carriage wheels. They also made the countless small metal pins, screws, and bolts that held the parts of the vehicle together. In many ways, the blacksmith's work held his community together, too.

FIVE

Many Smiths, Many Skills

In the colonial countryside, a village or plantation might have only one blacksmith who worked alone with his apprentices. This blacksmith became a jack-of-all-trades. The community relied on him to make and fix everything from teakettles to pickaxes to the pieces for a decorative fence. But colonial towns were usually large enough to support several blacksmiths. Demand for blacksmiths was so high in the city of Philadelphia that more than fifty master blacksmiths kept shop there in 1774. With so much competition, young blacksmiths usually became specialists. Instead of making every kind of iron object, they focused on one type of product. Colonists could visit the shop of a cutler or gunsmith to buy knives and guns used for warfare, protection, or hunting. Nailsmiths produced the huge numbers of nails needed for building and ship construction.

More Metals

Some smiths specialized by working with metals other than iron and steel. Wealthy colonists liked the look of pewter, a metal that combines tin with copper or lead. They bought pewter candlesticks, serving platters, and water pitchers. Spoons were often made of pewter, as were buttons. The pewterer did not pound out his metal. Instead, he carved a mold from wood or clay. Pewter was melted in an iron jug and poured into the mold. When it cooled, the mold was broken or pried opened to remove the object. Coppersmiths, silversmiths, and tinsmiths could also be found in colonial cities. They made a variety of useful and ornamental objects that were found in colonial homes.

The Farrier

The average colonist rode his horse when traveling long distances. When the family traveled, they used a carriage or wagon pulled by one or more horses. Farmers depended on horses and oxen to drag their heavy plows across the fields. There were no trains or trucks in colonial America, so these animals were also used for long-distance transportation. But the constant travel on hard-packed roads was hard on their feet. As protection, horses and oxen were fitted with thick iron shoes.

Tin Punch Ornament

The colonial tinsmith specialized in forging useful items for the home, such as tin eating utensils and candlesticks. Tinsmiths often used a technique called punching, which involved making small holes in the metal. Many lanterns were made by punching holes in a sheet of tin and then welding the piece into a box or tube shape. When a candle was lit inside, light streamed out of the holes. Creative tinsmiths made their punches in a pattern. Many colonial homes were brightened by these decorative touches. Make sure to have an adult help you with this project.

Things You Will Need

- a clean aluminum pie plate
- tracing paper
- a pencil
- scissors
- a permanent marker
- stencils of your choice
- cardboard (as large as the pie plate; thicker is better)
- a small, clean nail
- a hammer
- yarn or string

Instructions:

1. Place the pie plate on a table, with the open side down. Rest a sheet of tracing paper over the bottom of the plate.

2. Using the pencil, trace a line on the paper to match the bottom of the plate. Cut out the circle.

3. Choose a stencil design that you like. Use a pencil to trace the design onto the paper. (You can also draw your own pattern, but it should not be too complex.)

4. Put the paper back inside the pie plate. Using the permanent marker, make small dots along the lines of your pattern. The dots should be about one-quarter inch apart. When you remove the paper, you should see a dotted pattern on the aluminum.

5. Put the pie plate atop a piece of cardboard. (This protects the surface underneath from damage.) Take the nail and place it on one of the dots. Tap the nail with the hammer to punch through the plate. Watch your fingers! Repeat this until you have punched all of the holes.

6. Hold the plate up. Your pattern should be easy to see.

7. Make a last hole at the top of the plate. You can string a piece of yarn through the hole and hang your ornament in a window or on a wall.

The blacksmith often made horseshoes. To begin, he bent a band of iron until it formed a U shape. He then punched half a dozen holes into the metal. The shoe was measured against the bottom of the horse's hoof. If necessary, it could be adjusted—made wider or narrower, thicker or thinner. A better-fitting shoe helped the animal avoid injuries. The finished shoe was attached to the hoof by means of special horseshoe nails inserted through the holes and hammered into the fingernail-like material of the hoof wall. This caused no pain to the horse, but the shoe would stay on. Where necessary, blacksmiths also made special winter shoes. These had spikes on the bottom to prevent slipping on the ice.

Any blacksmith could make horseshoes, but the **farrier** offered much more. He was a specialized blacksmith trained to care for large farm animals. Colonists brought their horses and oxen in for regular checkups and called the farrier when an animal was ill. The farrier could calm even the most skittish horse with his quiet voice and gentle touch. When he had the horse's trust, he examined its feet and legs for injuries, trimmed its hooves to prevent painful sores, and put on shoes if that was the owner's wish. Finally, the farrier checked the horse's eyes, skin, and teeth to determine if it was healthy. He used a long metal rasp to file down any teeth that had become rough or broken. Good teeth meant a longer life for most horses.

As the blacksmith looks on, a farrier in Colonial Williamsburg attaches a new horseshoe to this horse's hoof.

Dr. Blacksmith

Some colonial villages were lucky enough to have an apothecary, a man who had all the skills of a doctor, surgeon, and pharmacist. He could treat illnesses and injuries, make medicines, and even provide dental care. But the apothecary's services were expensive. Colonists sometimes chose to treat their own illnesses rather than paying a fee. In desperate cases, they might visit the other medical expert in town—the farrier. The metal tongs he used to handle hot nails were perfect for the task of pulling infected teeth. Because he was used to working with excitable horses, the farrier was quick and careful in his work on human patients.

Colonists sent children to see the blacksmith when a youngster had a sty, or small swelling around the eye. The blacksmith calmly told the child to wait until he finished his work. During this time, the heat and steam of the smithy caused the child to blink and squint. Soon the sty had burst, and the blacksmith needed only to wipe the child's face clean. No surgery was required.

The Locksmith

Even in colonial times people were concerned about protecting their homes and belongings from theft. For this service they called on the locksmith, a specially trained blacksmith who built locks for doors, as well as for safes and other objects that held valuables.

Door locks were large, rectangular boxes made of iron or brass. Latches and doorknobs were attached to the outside of the box, and a bolt fit inside. When the key was inserted, this bolt could be turned to unlock the door. The locksmith started with a plain skeleton key—a rounded piece of iron up to 3 inches long with a "flag" of plain metal at its end. He shaved and cut the flag until it had a unique shape. Then he built a special bolt to fit the key and a box to fit around the bolt. Because each key was different, it was harder for a thief to pick any one lock.

A door lock was helpful, but it didn't keep out every robber. Colonists also needed something in which to store their important papers, jewels, and cash. Many chose to use money chests. These were usually made of wood planks held together by strong iron hinges. The locksmith manufactured large metal padlocks to hold these hinges shut. Colonial governments also used chests to protect their money. They ordered special safe boxes made entirely of iron. For these, the locksmith made padlocks plus a third lock that was built right into the lid. The keys were given to different people. If a thief wanted to break into a government money chest, he had to get all three keys.

The Battle for America

England's colonies in the New World were started by small groups of people who struggled to make their way under challenging conditions. Hard work and a constant stream of new immigrants helped the colonies to thrive. By 1770 the European population in America had increased to more than 2.1 million. Farms and plantations, villages and cities were spread along the Atlantic coastline from Maine to Georgia. This thriving collection of thirteen colonies was still ruled by Great Britain. But America had already started to become a melting pot of people. The colonies were home to immigrants from many European nations and slaves who had been brought from different parts of Africa. Where they could, American Indians continued to live near their traditional homes.

As America grew, some colonists began to clamor for independence. These patriots did not want to follow laws made by a distant king, nor did they like paying taxes to his government. They began to plan a revolution. Other colonists continued to

A colonial blacksmith forges weapons during the Revolutionary War.

support the king and his government. Known as Loyalists, they refused to rebel. Many other people were unsure what to believe or which side to support.

Blacksmiths could not avoid the situation. Patriots and Loyalists both called on blacksmiths to provide the weapons, horseshoes, and many other supplies needed for war. And when the war began in 1775, even the specialists—farriers, nailsmiths, and locksmiths—packed up their tools and joined the troops as they marched off to battle. Whichever side they supported, blacksmiths fought to protect the colonies they had helped to build.

Glossary

anvil	a heavy iron and steel block on which a blacksmith places metal to be hammered
apprentice	a person who trains to learn a new skill or job by working with an expert
bellows	a device that can be pumped to push air into a fire or forge
blast furnace	a tall steel tube lined with bricks, in which iron ore is smelted
bog iron	iron ore that is found in swamps
charcoal	burned wood that can be used to heat a forge or other fire
craftsmen	workers who have trained to learn special skills
farrier	a blacksmith who works with animals
forge	a furnace in a blacksmith's shop, where iron and other metals are heated
indenture	a contract requiring a person to serve an employer for a period of years, as a worker or apprentice
journeyman	a trained blacksmith who works to gain experience
ore	a rock that contains metal
shipwright	a craftsman who builds or repairs ships
smelting	using heat to remove metal from an ore
smite	to pound or hammer (source of the word *smith*)
swage	a block-shaped anvil used to round or bend pieces of metal
weld	to join pieces of metal by heating or hammering them

Find Out More

BOOKS

Hakim, Joy. *Making Thirteen Colonies*. New York: Oxford University Press, 2007.

Kalman, Bobbie. *A Visual Dictionary of a Colonial Community*. New York: Crabtree Publishing Company, 2008.

Landau, Elaine. *Explore Jamestown with Elaine Landau*. Berkeley Heights, NJ: Enslow Elementary, 2006.

Lange, Karen. *1607: A New Look at Jamestown*. Washington, D.C.: National Geographic Children's Books, 2007.

Love, Rebecca. *English Colonies in America*. Mankato, MN: Compass Point Books, 2008.

Mara, Wil. *The Silversmith*. New York: Marshall Cavendish Benchmark, 2010.

Winter, Kay, and Larry Day. *Colonial Voices: Hear Them Speak*. New York: Dutton Juvenile, 2008.

WEBSITES

A Day in the Life—An Apprentice's Life

www.history.org/History/teaching/DaySeries/webactivities/apprentice/1_4.htm

Use this interactive site to find out more about the life of a blacksmith's apprentice in colonial America.

Colonial Williamsburg Kids Zone

www.history.org/kids/

Tour the colonial capital of Virginia and meet some of its important residents. There are games, activities, and many resources about colonial life and history.

Makers and Fixers

www.nysm.nysed.gov/albany/makers.html#makers

This site contains information about blacksmiths and other tradesmen in colonial Albany, New York.

Mount Vernon Blacksmith Shop

www.mountvernon.org/lcarn/pres_arch/index.cfm/555/98/

Learn about the restoration of a blacksmith's shop that once served the plantation of President George Washington.

Work in Colonial America

www.learnnc.org/lp/editions/nchist-colonial/5998

Watch video of a modern blacksmith who works in the colonial tradition.

Index

About the Author

Christine Petersen has written more than three dozen books and several magazine articles for a variety of audiences, from emerging readers to adults. Her subjects include science, nature, and social studies. When she's not writing, Petersen and her young son enjoy exploring the natural areas near their home in Minneapolis, Minnesota. She is a member of the Society of Children's Book Writers and Illustrators.